COLOR DICTIONARY

800 COLOR SHADES & SWATCHES COMPILATION

The aim of this book is **to inspire you** to find colors that are linked to a particular name. Each color includes its name so that it can serve as a reference for you.

Please note that the shade of the color may vary from one place to another and here we have chosen the ones we have considered the most accurate.

Each main color (White, Yellow, Orange, Red, Pink, Purple, Blue, Green, Brown & Black) **contains 80 shades.**

Check the HEX code (#) or RGB to use them digitally.

Bonus **Gift**

Scan the QR code and **receive the Guide in PDF format in which you can answer 20 questions to select the colors for your project without making a mistake.**

SCAN THIS QR CODE
WITH YOUR SMARTPHONE CAMERA

INDEX

WHITE

PURITY

INNOCENCE

LIGHT

CLEANLINESS

FAITH

SPIRITUALITY

SIMPLICITY

MINIMALISM

PROTECTION

SOFTNESS

PERFECTION

Acadia white
HEX #F4EFE3
RGB 244, 239, 227

Alabaster
HEX #EDEADE
RGB 237, 234, 222

Albescent white
HEX #F3DECA
RGB 243, 222, 202

Anti-Flash
HEX #F2F3F4
RGB 242, 243, 244

Atrium white
HEX #F1EEE4
RGB 241, 238, 228

Audience anger
HEX #EAF4FC
RGB 234, 244, 252

Baby powder
HEX #FEFEFA
RGB 254, 254, 250

Blanched almond
HEX #FFEBCD
RGB 255, 235, 205

Bone white
HEX #F9F6EE
RGB 249, 246, 238

Broken white
HEX #EEEBE3
RGB 238, 235, 227

Bubbles
HEX #E7FEFF
RGB 231, 254, 255

Cascading white
HEX #F7F5F6
RGB 247, 245, 246

Ceramic
HEX #FCFFF9
RGB 252, 255, 249

Chiffon
HEX #FFFACD
RGB 255, 250, 205

Cotton Ball
HEX #F2F7FD
RGB 242, 247, 253

Cough mixture
HEX #F6F4F1
RGB 246, 244, 241

Cup Cake
HEX #EBF6F7
RGB 235, 246, 247

Daisy
HEX #FAFAFA
RGB 250, 250, 250

Decorator's white
HEX #ECEFEC
RGB 236, 239, 236

Dutch white
HEX #EFDFBB
RGB 239, 223, 187

Eggshell
HEX #F0EAD6
RGB 240, 234, 214

Feather white
HEX #E7EAE5
RGB 231, 234, 229

Floral white
HEX #FFFAF0
RGB 255, 250, 240

Frost
HEX #FCFBFC
RGB 252, 251, 252

Gainsboro
HEX #DCDCDC
RGB 220, 220, 220

Ghost white
HEX #F8F8FF
RGB 248, 248, 255

Glitter
HEX #E6E8FA
RGB 230, 232, 250

Greek villa
HEX #F0EBE3
RGB 240, 235, 227

Half and half
HEX #FFFFE4
RGB 255, 255, 228

Harp
HEX #EBF5F0
RGB 235, 245, 240

Hog bristle quarter
HEX #EBE4D8
RGB 235, 228, 216

Honeydew
HEX #F0FFF0
RGB 240, 255, 240

3

Isabelline
HEX #F4F0EC
RGB 244, 240, 236

Island spice
HEX #FFFCEC
RGB 255, 252, 236

Lexicon
HEX #E7EAEA
RGB 231, 234, 234

Linen
HEX #E9DCC9
RGB 233, 220, 201

Link white
HEX #ECF3F9
RGB 236, 243, 249

Magnolia
HEX #F2E8D7
RGB 242, 232, 215

Mercury
HEX #E7E7E7
RGB 231, 231, 231

Merino
HEX #F2EBDD
RGB 242, 235, 221

Milk
HEX #FDFFF5
RGB 253, 255, 245

Mint cream
HEX #F5FFFA
RGB 245, 255, 250

Moon glow
HEX #F4F1C9
RGB 244, 241, 201

Moon white
HEX #F4F6F0
RGB 244, 246, 240

Natural white
HEX #EEECE6
RGB 238, 236, 230

Navajo white
HEX #FFDEAD
RGB 255, 222, 173

Off white
HEX #FAF9F6
RGB 250, 249, 246

Old lace
HEX #FDF5E6
RGB 253, 245, 230

Old wood
HEX #F0EEE4
RGB 240, 238, 228

Oyster white
HEX #E3DFD2
RGB 227, 223, 210

Parchment
HEX #FCF5E5
RGB 252, 245, 229

Pearl
HEX #E2DFD2
RGB 226, 223, 210

Peppermint
HEX #F1F9EC
RGB 241, 249, 236

Photon white
HEX #F8F8E8
RGB 248, 248, 232

Pink salt
HEX #F8EEEC
RGB 248, 238, 236

Platinum
HEX #E5E4E2
RGB 229, 228, 226

Polar bear
HEX #EAE9E0
RGB 234, 233, 224

Pomelo white
HEX F9FFE3
RGB 249, 255, 227

Powder
HEX #FBFCFA
RGB 251, 252, 250

Rice
HEX #FAF5EF
RGB 250, 245, 239

Rose white
HEX #FFFAFA
RGB 255, 250, 250

Shadow white
HEX #EEF1EA
RGB 238, 241, 234

Simply white
HEX #EFEDE3
RGB 239, 237, 227

Snow
HEX #FFFAFA
RGB 255, 250, 250

Spatial white
HEX #DEDDDB
RGB 222, 221, 219

Swan
HEX #FCFCFC
RGB 252, 252, 252

Timberwolf
HEX #DBD7D2
RGB 219, 215, 210

Titan white
HEX #EEEEFF
RGB 238, 238, 255

Unresolved problem
HEX #F3F2ED
RGB 243, 242, 237

Vista white
HEX #FDFCFA
RGB 253, 252, 250

Vivid white
HEX #F8F8F4
RGB 248, 248, 244

White chocolate
HEX #EDE6D6
RGB 237, 230, 214

White diamond
HEX #E7E8E2
RGB 231, 232, 226

White dove
HEX #F0EFE7
RGB 240, 239, 231

White heat
HEX #FDF9EF
RGB 253, 249, 239

White on white
HEX #EDEFEF
RGB 237, 239, 239

White smoke
HEX #F5F5F5
RGB 245, 245, 245

White wisp
HEX #E9E9E4
RGB 233, 233, 228

Whitewash
HEX #FEFFFC
RGB 254, 255, 252

Winter white
HEX #DFDFD5
RGB 223, 223, 213

YELLOW

CHEERFULNESS

ENTHUSIASM

FUN

CONFIDENCE

ORIGINALITY

CREATIVITY

CHALLENGING

ACADEMIC

WISDOM

LOGIC

Sunglow
HEX **#FFCC33**
RGB **255, 204, 51**

Amber
HEX #FFBF00
RGB 255, 191, 0

Apricot
HEX #FBCEB1
RGB 251, 206, 177

Arylide yellow
HEX #E9D66B
RGB 233, 214, 107

Aureolin
HEX #FDEE00
RGB 253, 238, 0

Banana
HEX #FFE135
RGB 255, 225, 53

Beige
HEX #F5F5DC
RGB 245, 245, 220

Blazing yellow
HEX #FEE715
RGB 254, 231, 21

Brass
HEX #E1C16E
RGB 225, 193, 110

Bright Yellow
HEX #FFEA00
RGB 255, 234, 0

Bumblebee
HEX #FCE205
RGB 252, 226, 5

Butter
HEX #FFFD74
RGB 255, 253, 116

Cadmium yellow
HEX #FFFF8F
RGB 255, 255, 143

Citrine
HEX #E4D00A
RGB 228, 208, 10

Citron
HEX #DDD06A
RGB 221, 208, 106

Cornsilk
HEX #FFF8DC
RGB 255, 248, 220

Cosmic latte
HEX #FFF8E7
RGB 255, 248, 231

Cream
HEX #FFFDD0
RGB 255, 253, 208

Cyber yellow
HEX #FFD300
RGB 255, 211, 0

Daisy yellow
HEX #F8DC75
RGB 248, 220, 117

Dandelion
HEX #F0E130
RGB 240, 225, 48

Dark goldenrod
HEX #B8860B
RGB 184, 134, 11

Dark yellow
HEX #D5B60A
RGB 213, 182, 10

Dull yellow
HEX #DECA57
RGB 222, 202, 87

Ecru
HEX #C2B280
RGB 194, 178, 128

Flax
HEX #EEDC82
RGB 238, 220, 130

Gamboge
HEX #E49B0F
RGB 228, 155, 15

Gold
HEX #FFD700
RGB 255, 215, 0

Golden yellow
HEX #FFC000
RGB 255, 192, 0

Goldenrod
HEX #DAA520
RGB 218, 165, 32

Harvest gold
HEX #E6A817
RGB 230, 168, 23

Hot yellow
HEX #FFDA00
RGB 255, 218, 0

Icterine
HEX #FCF55F
RGB 252, 245, 95

Ivory
HEX #FFFFF0
RGB 255, 255, 240

Jasmine
HEX #F8DE7E
RGB 248, 222, 126

Khaki
HEX #F0E68C
RGB 240, 230, 140

Laguna
HEX #F8E473
RGB 248, 228, 115

Lemon chiffon
HEX #FFFACD
RGB 255, 250, 205

Lemon yellow
HEX #FFF44F
RGB 255, 244, 79

Lemon-lime
HEX #E3FF00
RGB 227, 255, 0

Light yellow
HEX #FFFFE0
RGB 255, 255, 224

Lion
HEX #DECC9C
RGB 222, 204, 156

Maize
HEX #FBEC5D
RGB 251, 236, 93

Mango
HEX #F4BB44
RGB 244, 187, 68

Maximum
HEX #FAFA37
RGB 250, 250, 55

Mellow yellow
HEX #F8DE7E
RGB 248, 222, 126

Metallic gold
HEX #D4AF37
RGB 212, 175, 55

Mikado yellow
HEX #FFC40C
RGB 255, 196, 12

Mustard yellow
HEX #FFDB58
RGB 255, 219, 88

Muted yellow
HEX #E0D268
RGB 224, 210, 104

Naples yellow
HEX #FADA5E
RGB 250, 218, 94

Nyanza
HEX #ECFFDC
RGB 236, 255, 220

Pale yellow
HEX #FFFFA7
RGB 255, 255, 167

Pastel yellow
HEX #FFFAA0
RGB 255, 250, 160

Peach
HEX #FFE5B4
RGB 255, 229, 180

Pear
HEX #C9CC3F
RGB 201, 204, 63

Peridot
HEX #DFEC4A
RGB 223, 236, 74

Pineapple
HEX #FEEA63
RGB 254, 234, 99

Psychedelic
HEX #FFF53D
RGB 255, 245, 61

Radioactive
HEX #FAE500
RGB 250, 229, 0

Rainbow yellow
HEX #F5DE10
RGB 245, 222, 16

Royal yellow
HEX #FADA5E
RGB 250, 218, 94

Safety yellow
HEX #EED202
RGB 238, 210, 2

Saffron
HEX #F4C430
RGB 244, 196, 48

Sandstorm
HEX #ECD540
RGB 236, 213, 64

School bus
HEX #FFD800
RGB 255, 216, 0

Stil de grain
HEX #FADA5E
RGB 250, 218, 94

Straw
HEX #E4D96F
RGB 228, 217, 111

Sulfur
HEX #E8DE35
RGB 232, 222, 53

Sunflower
HEX #FFDA03
RGB 255, 218, 3

Sunglow
HEX #FFCC33
RGB 255, 204, 51

Trombone
HEX #D2B55B
RGB 210, 181, 91

Unmellow yellow
HEX #FFFF66
RGB 255, 255, 102

Vanilla
HEX #F3E5AB
RGB 243, 229, 171

Vegas Gold
HEX #C4B454
RGB 196, 180, 84

Vibrant yellow
HEX #FFDA29
RGB 255, 218, 41

Wheat
HEX #F5DEB3
RGB 245, 222, 179

Xanthic
HEX #EEED09
RGB 238, 237, 9

Yellow orange
HEX #FFAA33
RGB 255, 170, 51

Yellow canary
HEX #FFEF00
RGB 255, 239, 0

Yolk yellow
HEX #E2B051
RGB 226, 176, 81

ORANGE

ENTHUSIASTIC

SELF-CONFIDENT

INDEPENDENT

EXTRAVERTED

ADVENTUROUS

RISK-TAKER

INFORMAL

HAPPINES

OPTIMISM

MOTIVATION

Pumpkin
HEX **#F5761A**
RGB 245, 118, 26

Aerospace orange
HEX #FF4F00
RGB 255, 79, 0

Aesthetic orange
HEX #F4AB6A
RGB 244, 171, 106

Alloy orange
HEX #C46210
RGB 196, 98, 16

Atomic tangerine
HEX #FF9966
RGB 255, 153, 102

Beer orange
HEX #F28F1C
RGB 242, 143, 28

Bright orange
HEX #FFAC1C
RGB 255, 172, 28

Browns orange
HEX #FF3C00
RGB 255, 60, 0

Bumblebee orange
HEX #FFC82A
RGB 255, 200, 42

Burnt orange
HEX #CC5500
RGB 204, 85, 0

Butterscotch
HEX #E3963E
RGB 227, 150, 62

Cadmium orange
HEX #F28C28
RGB 242, 140, 40

Calm
HEX #FAB972
RGB 250, 185, 114

Carrot
HEX #ED9121
RGB 237, 145, 33

Champagne
HEX #F7E7CE
RGB 247, 231, 206

Cheese orange
HEX #FFA600
RGB 255, 166, 0

Chinese orange
HEX #EB6841
RGB 235, 104, 65

Cider orange
HEX #EB6841
RGB 235, 104, 65

Coral
HEX #FF7F50
RGB 255, 127, 80

Dark orange
HEX #DC582A
RGB 220,88,42

Dark topaz orange
HEX #EABD8C
RGB 234, 189, 140

Desert
HEX #FAD5A5
RGB 250, 213, 165

Dragon fire orange
HEX #FD652D
RGB 253, 101, 45

Dutch orange
HEX #FF9B00
RGB 255, 155, 0

Flame
HEX #E25822
RGB 226, 88, 34

Glossy
HEX #E78400
RGB 231, 132, 0

Goldfish orange
HEX #FF9913
RGB 255, 153, 19

Halloween orange
HEX #EE5921
RGB 238, 89, 33

Hot orange
HEX #FF6E00
RGB 255, 110, 0

India saffron
HEX #FF9933
RGB 255, 153, 51

International orange
HEX #FF4F00
RGB 255, 79, 0

Irish orange
HEX #F5883F
RGB 245, 136, 63

Jasper orange
HEX #E89149
RGB 232, 145, 73

Koi orange
HEX #D15837
RGB 209, 88, 55

Lava orange
HEX #F76806
RGB 247, 104, 6

Light orange
HEX #FFD580
RGB 255, 213, 128

Mango tango
HEX #FB8842
RGB 251, 136, 66

Marigold orange
HEX #EAA221
RGB 234, 162, 33

Marmalade
HEX #D16002
RGB 209, 96, 2

Mecca
HEX #BD5745
RGB 189, 87, 69

Mimosa orange
HEX #FFCA4B
RGB 255, 202, 75

Neon orange
HEX #FF5F1F
RGB 255, 95, 31

Orange pale
HEX #FFDFBF
RGB 255, 223, 191

Orange paper
HEX #FEE8D6
RGB 254, 232, 214

Orange peel
HEX #FF9F00
RGB 255, 159, 0

Outrageous
HEX #FF6E4A
RGB 255, 110, 74

Papaya whip
HEX #FFEFD5
RGB 255, 239, 213

Pastel orange
HEX #FAC898
RGB 250, 200, 152

Pepper orange
HEX #E77D22
RGB 231, 125, 34

Persian orange
HEX #D99058
RGB 217, 144, 88

Persimmon
HEX #EC5800
RGB 236, 88, 0

Pumpkin
HEX #F5761A
RGB 245, 118, 26

Pure orange
HEX #FF8000
RGB 255, 128, 0

Rajah
HEX #FABA5F
RGB 250, 186, 95

Red orange
HEX #FF4433
RGB 255, 68, 51

Royal orange
HEX #FF9944
RGB 255, 153, 68

Rumba
HEX #F06631
RGB 240, 102, 49

Rustic
HEX #D78C3D
RGB 215, 140, 61

Safety orange
HEX #FF5F15
RGB 255, 95, 21

Safflower
HEX #FDAE44
RGB 253, 174, 68

Salamander
HEX #F05E23
RGB 240, 94, 35

Salmon
HEX #FF8066
RGB 255, 128, 102

Smashed pumpkin
HEX #FD673A
RGB 253, 103, 58

Spanish orange
HEX #E86100
RGB 232, 97, 0

Spice orange
HEX #D76B00
RGB 215, 107, 0

Squash
HEX #E89362
RGB 232, 147, 98

Sunrise orange
HEX #E67451
RGB 230, 116, 81

Sunset orange
HEX #FA5F55
RGB 250, 95, 85

Tangelo
HEX #F94D00
RGB 249,77,0

Tangerine
HEX #F08000
RGB 240, 128, 0

Tiger
HEX #F96815
RGB 249, 104, 21

Tiger's eye
HEX #E08D3C
RGB 224, 141, 60

Tree Sap
HEX #CC7711
RGB 204, 119, 17

Vermilion
HEX #D74826
RGB 215, 72, 38

Vivid orange
HEX #FF5E0E
RGB 255, 94, 14

Web orange
HEX #FFA500
RGB 255, 165, 0

West Side orange
HEX #FF9916
RGB 255, 153, 22

Wheat orange
HEX #F5DEB3
RGB 245, 222, 179

Willpower
HEX #FD5602
RGB 253, 86, 2

Xanthous
HEX #F1B42F
RGB 241, 180, 47

Yam orange
HEX #E17E45
RGB 225, 126, 69

RED

LOVE

SEDUCTION

SEXUALITY

DESIRE

VIOLENCE

DANGER

ANGER

ACTION

JOY

STRENGTH

HEAT

Lust
HEX **#E62020**
RGB **230, 32, 32**

Alizarin crimson
HEX #E32636
RGB 227, 38, 54

American
HEX #FF033E
RGB 255, 3, 62

Barn red
HEX #7C0902
RGB 124, 9, 2

Bittersweet
HEX #FE6F5E
RGB 254, 111, 94

Bittersweet shimmer
HEX #BF4F51
RGB 191, 79, 81

Blood red
HEX #660000
RGB 102, 0, 0

Brick red
HEX #AA4A44
RGB 170, 74, 68

Bright red
HEX #EE4B2B
RGB 238, 75, 43

Burgundy
HEX #800020
RGB 128, 0, 32

Burnt umber
HEX #6E260E
RGB 110, 38, 14

Cadmium red
HEX #D22B2B
RGB 210, 43, 43

Candy apple red
HEX #FF0800
RGB 255, 8, 0

Carmine
HEX #960018
RGB 150, 0, 24

Carnelian red
HEX #B31B1B
RGB 179, 27, 27

Cherry
HEX #D2042D
RGB 210, 4, 45

Chestnut
HEX #954535
RGB 149, 69, 53

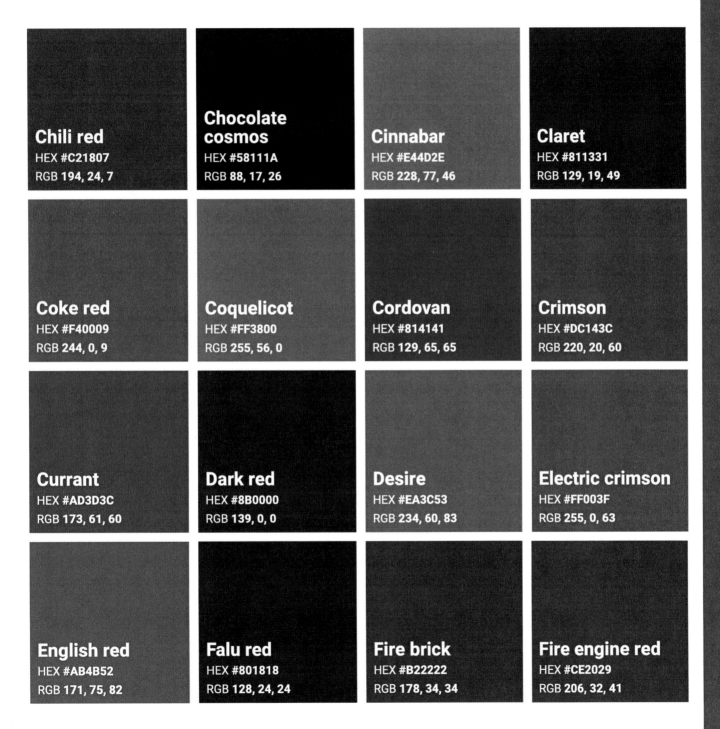

Chili red
HEX #C21807
RGB 194, 24, 7

Chocolate cosmos
HEX #58111A
RGB 88, 17, 26

Cinnabar
HEX #E44D2E
RGB 228, 77, 46

Claret
HEX #811331
RGB 129, 19, 49

Coke red
HEX #F40009
RGB 244, 0, 9

Coquelicot
HEX #FF3800
RGB 255, 56, 0

Cordovan
HEX #814141
RGB 129, 65, 65

Crimson
HEX #DC143C
RGB 220, 20, 60

Currant
HEX #AD3D3C
RGB 173, 61, 60

Dark red
HEX #8B0000
RGB 139, 0, 0

Desire
HEX #EA3C53
RGB 234, 60, 83

Electric crimson
HEX #FF003F
RGB 255, 0, 63

English red
HEX #AB4B52
RGB 171, 75, 82

Falu red
HEX #801818
RGB 128, 24, 24

Fire brick
HEX #B22222
RGB 178, 34, 34

Fire engine red
HEX #CE2029
RGB 206, 32, 41

Flame red
HEX #E25822
RGB 226, 88, 34

Folly red
HEX #FF004F
RGB 255, 0, 79

Fuzzy Wuzzy red
HEX #CC6666
RGB 204, 102, 102

Garnet
HEX #9A2A2A
RGB 154, 42, 42

Hibiscus
HEX #B43757
RGB 180, 55, 87

Imperial Red
HEX #ED2939
RGB 237, 41, 57

Indian Red
HEX #CD5C5C
RGB 205, 92, 92

Japanese carmine
HEX #9D2933
RGB 157, 41, 51

Jasper
HEX #D05340
RGB 208, 83, 64

Jasper Red
HEX #D73B3E
RGB 215, 59, 62

Jelly bean red
HEX #DA614E
RGB 218, 97, 78

Lava red
HEX #CF1020
RGB 207, 16, 32

Light coral
HEX #F08080
RGB 240, 128, 128

Lust
HEX #E62020
RGB 230, 32, 32

Madder
HEX #A50021
RGB 165, 0, 33

Mahogany
HEX #C04000
RGB 192, 64, 0

Maroon
HEX #800000
RGB 128, 0, 0

Marsala
HEX #986868
RGB 152, 104, 104

Merlot
HEX #7B3539
RGB 123, 52, 57

Minium
HEX #FF4101
RGB 255, 65, 1

Neon Red
HEX #FF3131
RGB 255, 49, 49

Oxblood
HEX #4A0404
RGB 74, 4, 4

Persian red
HEX #CC3333
RGB 204, 51, 51

Prismatic red
HEX #D03D33
RGB 208, 61, 51

Prismatic legacy
HEX #BA1607
RGB 186, 22, 7

Prune
HEX #701C1C
RGB 112, 28, 28

Poppy
HEX #E35335
RGB 227, 83, 53

Popstar
HEX #BE4F62
RGB 190, 79, 98

Puce
HEX #A95C68
RGB 169, 92, 104

Radical red
HEX #FF355E
RGB 255, 53, 94

Raspberry
HEX #E30B5C
RGB 227, 11, 92

Red brown
HEX #A52A2A
RGB 165, 42, 42

Red devil
HEX #860111
RGB 134, 1, 17

Red ochre
HEX #913831
RGB 145, 56, 49

Red salsa
HEX #FD3A4A
RGB 253, 58, 74

Redwood
HEX #A45953
RGB 164, 89, 83

Rusty red
HEX #DA2C43
RGB 218, 44, 67

Sangria
HEX #5E1914
RGB 94, 25, 20

Sanguine
HEX #BC3F4A
RGB 188, 63, 74

Scarlet
HEX #FF2400
RGB 255, 36, 0

Sundown
HEX #FAA0A0
RGB 250, 160, 160

Tango
HEX #E4717A
RGB 228, 113, 122

Terracotta
HEX #E3735E
RGB 227, 115, 94

Tomato
HEX #FF6347
RGB 255, 99, 71

Tractor
HEX #FD0E35
RGB 253, 14, 53

Turkey red
HEX #A91101
RGB 169, 17, 1

Tuscan red
HEX #7C3030
RGB 124, 48, 48

Venetian red
HEX #A42A04
RGB 164, 42, 4

PINK

COMPASSION

FEMINITY

PASSION

SWEET

ROMANCE

FAITHFULNESS

BEAUTY

CHILDISHNESS

FRIENDSHIP

SENSITIVITY

PLAYFUL

Rose
HEX **#F33A6A**
RGB **243, 58, 106**

Amaranth pink
HEX #F19CBB
RGB 241, 156, 187

Baby pink
HEX #F4C2C2
RGB 244, 194, 194

Baker-Miller
HEX #FF91AF
RGB 255, 145, 175

Bisque
HEX #F2D2BD
RGB 242, 210, 189

Blush
HEX #FE828C
RGB 254,130,140

Bright pink
HEX #FF007F
RGB 255, 0, 127

Brilliant rose
HEX #FF55A3
RGB 255, 85, 163

Brink
HEX #FF6090
RGB 255, 96, 144

Bubblegum
HEX #FFC1CC
RGB 255, 193, 204

Cameo pink
HEX #EFBBCC
RGB 239, 187, 204

Candy pink
HEX #E4717A
RGB 228, 113, 122

Carnation
HEX #FFA6C9
RGB 255, 166, 201

Cerise
HEX #DE3163
RGB 222, 49, 99

Cherry blossom
HEX #FFB7C5
RGB 255, 183, 197

Coral pink
HEX #F88379
RGB 248, 131, 121

Cotton candy
HEX #FFBCD9
RGB 255, 188, 217

Crepe
HEX #F89883
RGB 248, 152, 131

Cyclamen
HEX #F56FA1
RGB 245, 111, 161

Dark pink
HEX #AA336A
RGB 170, 51, 106

Dark terra cotta
HEX #CC4E5C
RGB 204, 78, 92

Deep pink
HEX #FF1493
RGB 255, 20, 147

Dogwood rose
HEX #D71868
RGB 215, 24, 104

Dusty rose
HEX #C9A9A6
RGB 201, 169, 166

Fairy tale
HEX #F2C1D1
RGB 242, 193, 209

Flamingo
HEX #FC8EAC
RGB 252, 142, 172

French pink
HEX #F64A8A
RGB 246, 74, 138

Hot pink
HEX #FF69B4
RGB 255, 105, 180

Lavender blush
HEX #FFF0F5
RGB 255, 240, 245

Lavender pink
HEX #FBAED2
RGB 251, 174, 210

Lemonade
HEX #F2DBE7
RGB 242, 219, 231

Light pink
HEX #FFB6C1
RGB 255, 182, 193

Magenta
HEX #FF00FF
RGB 255, 0, 255

Mexican pink
HEX #E4007C
RGB 228, 0, 124

Millennial pink
HEX #F3CFC6
RGB 243, 207, 198

Mimi pink
HEX #FFDAE9
RGB 255, 218, 233

Misty rose
HEX #FFE4E1
RGB 255, 228, 225

Nadeshiko pink
HEX #F6ADC6
RGB 246, 173, 198

Neon pink
HEX #FF10F0
RGB 255, 16, 240

New York pink
HEX #DD8374
RGB 221, 131, 116

Old rose
HEX #C08081
RGB 192, 128, 129

Orchid
HEX #DA70D6
RGB 218, 112, 214

Oyster
HEX #F0D8D8
RGB 240, 216, 216

Paradise Pink
HEX #E63E62
RGB 230, 62, 98

Pastel pink
HEX #F8C8DC
RGB 248, 200, 220

Persian pink
HEX #F77FBE
RGB 247, 127, 190

Piggy pink
HEX #FDDDE6
RGB 253, 221, 230

Pink orange
HEX #F89880
RGB 248, 152, 128

Pink pearl
HEX #E7ACCF
RGB 231, 172, 207

Pink sherbet
HEX #F78FA7
RGB 247, 143, 167

Plum
HEX #673147
RGB 103, 49, 71

Punch
HEX #F25278
RGB 242, 82, 120

Razzle dazzle rose
HEX #FF33CC
RGB 255, 51, 204

Razzmatazz
HEX #E3256B
RGB 227, 37, 107

Rose
HEX #F33A6A
RGB 243, 58, 106

Rose bonbon
HEX #F9429E
RGB 249, 66, 158

Rose Gold
HEX #E0BFB8
RGB 224, 191, 184

Rose pompadour
HEX #ED7A9B
RGB 237, 122, 155

Rose quartz
HEX #F7CACA
RGB 247, 202, 202

Ruby
HEX #E0115F
RGB 224, 17, 95

Ruddy pink
HEX #E18E96
RGB 225, 142, 150

Seashell
HEX #FFF5EE
RGB 255, 245, 238

Shampoo
HEX #FFCFF1
RGB 255, 207, 241

Shimmering blush
HEX #D98695
RGB 217, 134, 149

Shocking pink
HEX #FC0FC0
RGB 252, 15, 192

Spanish pink
HEX #F7BFBE
RGB 247, 191, 190

Steel pink
HEX #CC3366
RGB 204, 51, 102

Strawberry
HEX #E8888A
RGB 232, 136, 138

Super pink
HEX #CF6BA9
RGB 207, 107, 169

Taffy
HEX #FA86C4
RGB 250, 134, 196

Tea rose
HEX #F4C2C2
RGB 244, 194, 194

Telemagenta
HEX #CF3476
RGB 207, 52, 118

Thistle
HEX #D8BFD8
RGB 216, 191, 216

Tickle me pink
HEX #FC89AC
RGB 252, 137, 172

Tulip pink
HEX #FF8E8E
RGB 255, 142, 142

Ultra pink
HEX #FF6FFF
RGB 255, 111, 255

Valentine pink
HEX #E6A6BE
RGB 230, 166, 190

Vanilla ice
HEX #F38FA9
RGB 243, 143, 169

Watermelon pink
HEX #E37383
RGB 227, 115, 131

Wild strawberry
HEX #FF43A4
RGB 255, 67, 164

Your
HEX #FFC0C0
RGB 255, 192, 192

PURPLE

ROYALTY

LUXURY

MYSTERY

AMBITION

EXTRAVAGANCE

INTUITIVE

POWER

NOBILITY

REPENTANCE

FANTASY

WEALTH

Amethyst
HEX **#9966CC**
RGB **153, 102, 204**

Affair
HEX #6F4685
RGB 111, 70, 133

African violet
HEX #B284BE
RGB 178, 132, 190

Amaranth
HEX #9F2B68
RGB 159, 43, 104

Amethyst
HEX #9966CC
RGB 153, 102, 204

Boss's jokes
HEX #B0306A
RGB 176, 48, 106

Bright purple
HEX #BF40BF
RGB 191, 64, 191

Byzantium
HEX #702963
RGB 112, 41, 99

Chinese violet
HEX #856088
RGB 133, 96, 136

Dark magenta
HEX #8B008B
RGB 139, 0, 139

Dark purple
HEX #301934
RGB 48, 25, 52

Dark violet
HEX #9400D3
RGB 148, 0, 211

Early bird
HEX #CEA2FD
RGB 206, 162, 253

Eggplant
HEX #483248
RGB 72, 50, 72

Electric purple
HEX #BF00FF
RGB 191, 0, 255

Eminence
HEX #6C3082
RGB 108, 48, 130

English violet
HEX #563C5C
RGB 86, 60, 92

Fandango
HEX #B53389
RGB 181, 51, 137

French mauve
HEX #D473D4
RGB 212, 115, 212

Fuchsia
HEX #FF00FF
RGB 255, 0, 255

Good tax
HEX #C9A0FF
RGB 201, 160, 255

Grape
HEX #6F2DA8
RGB 111, 45, 168

Heather
HEX #9E7BB5
RGB 158, 123, 181

Heliotrope
HEX #DF73FF
RGB 223, 115, 255

Hopbush
HEX #D05FAD
RGB 208, 95, 173

Imperial purple
HEX #602F6B
RGB 96, 47, 107

Indigo
HEX #4B0082
RGB 75, 0, 130

Iris
HEX #5D3FD3
RGB 93, 63, 211

Jam
HEX #67032F
RGB 103, 3, 47

Kalamata
HEX #705160
RGB 112, 81, 96

Kingfisher daisy
HEX #653780
RGB 101, 55, 128

Lavender light
HEX #E6E6FA
RGB 230, 230, 250

Light Purple
HEX #CF9FFF
RGB 207, 159, 255

Lilac
HEX #AA98A9
RGB 170, 152, 169

Lipstick stain
HEX #8E4785
RGB 142, 71, 133

Liserian purple
HEX #DE6FA1
RGB 222, 111, 161

Long distance
HEX #6F456E
RGB 111, 69, 110

Lovely purple
HEX #7F38EC
RGB 127, 56, 236

Mardi gras
HEX #880085
RGB 136, 0, 133

Mauve
HEX #E0B0FF
RGB 224, 176, 255

Mauve taupe
HEX #915F6D
RGB 145, 95, 109

Mauveine
HEX #8D029B
RGB 141,2,155

Medium purple
HEX #9370DB
RGB 147, 112, 219

Mountain's majesty
HEX #9078C0
RGB 144, 120, 192

Mulberry
HEX #770737
RGB 119, 7, 55

Munsell purple
HEX #9F00C5
RGB 159, 0, 197

Palatinate
HEX #72246C
RGB 114, 36, 108

Pale purple
HEX #FAE6FA
RGB 250, 230, 250

Pansy purple
HEX #78184A
RGB 120, 24, 74

Pastel purple
HEX #C3B1E1
RGB 195, 177, 225

Pearly purple
HEX #B768A2
RGB 183, 104, 162

Phlox
HEX #DF00FF
RGB 223, 0, 255

Pizza edge
HEX #9A2CA0
RGB 154, 44, 160

Pomp and power
HEX #86608E
RGB 134, 96, 142

Pompadour
HEX #720058
RGB 114, 0, 88

Prince charming
HEX #493F5E
RGB 73, 63, 94

Purple heart
HEX #7442C8
RGB 116, 66, 200

Purple pizzazz
HEX #FE4EDA
RGB 254, 78, 218

Purpureus
HEX #9A4EAE
RGB 154, 78, 174

Quartz
HEX #51414F
RGB 81, 65, 79

Raisin
HEX #290916
RGB 41, 9, 22

Razzmic berry purple
HEX #8D4E85
RGB 141, 78, 133

Red purple
HEX #953553
RGB 149, 53, 83

Regalia purple
HEX #522D80
RGB 82, 45, 128

Ripe plum
HEX #410056
RGB 65, 0, 86

Royal purple
HEX #7851A9
RGB 120, 81, 169

Seance
HEX #61346B
RGB 97, 52, 107

Shiny purple
HEX #B941FF
RGB 185, 65, 255

Spanish violet
HEX #4C2882
RGB 76, 40, 130

Studio
HEX #7851A9
RGB 120, 81, 169

Tacao
HEX #6F3096
RGB 111, 48, 150

Traditional purple
HEX #8E4585
RGB 142, 69, 133

Traffic purple
HEX #913073
RGB 145, 48, 115

True purple
HEX #6A0DAD
RGB 106, 13, 173

Tyrian purple
HEX #630330
RGB 99, 3, 48

Ultra violet
HEX #645394
RGB 100, 83, 148

Veronica
HEX #A020F0
RGB 160, 32, 240

Violet
HEX #7F00FF
RGB 127, 0, 255

Wine
HEX #722F37
RGB 114, 47, 55

Wine dregs
HEX #673147
RGB 103, 49, 71

Wisteria
HEX #BDB5D5
RGB 189, 181, 213

BLUE

TRUST

PEACE

LOYALTY

COMPETENCE

IDEALISTIC

LONELINESS

CALM

RESPONSIBLE

HONESTY

RELAXING

SECURITY

Cobalt
HEX **#0047AB**
RGB **0, 71, 171**

Aegean Blue
HEX #4E6E81
RGB 78, 110, 129

Aero
HEX #00B9E8
RGB 0, 185, 232

Alice blue
HEX #F0F8FF
RGB 240, 248, 255

Aqua blue
HEX #05C3DD
RGB 5,195,221

Aquamarine
HEX #6BCAE2
RGB 107, 202, 226

Arctic
HEX #C6E6FB
RGB 198, 230, 251

Azure
HEX #F0FFFF
RGB 240, 255, 255

Baby blue
HEX #89CFF0
RGB 137, 207, 240

Berry
HEX #4F86F7
RGB 79, 134, 247

Bleu de France
HEX #318CE7
RGB 49, 140, 231

Blue gray
HEX #7393B3
RGB 115, 147, 179

Blue-gray
HEX #6699CC
RGB 102, 153, 204

Bondy blue
HEX #0095b6
RGB 0,149,182

Bright blue
HEX #0096FF
RGB 0, 150, 255

Byzantine
HEX #3457D5
RGB 52, 87, 213

Cadet
HEX #5F9EA0
RGB 95, 158, 160

Capri blue
HEX #00BFFF
RGB 0, 191, 255

Celestial
HEX #4997D0
RGB 73, 151, 208

Celtic
HEX #246BCE
RGB 36, 107, 206

Cerulean
HEX #007BA7
RGB 0, 123, 167

Chefchaouen
HEX #468FEA
RGB 70, 143, 234

Chlorine
HEX #0CAFFF
RGB 12, 175, 255

Cobalt
HEX #0047AB
RGB 0, 71, 171

Cornflower
HEX #6495ED
RGB 100, 149, 237

Cyan
HEX #00FFFF
RGB 0, 255, 255

Dark blue
HEX #00008B
RGB 0, 0, 139

Deep sky
HEX #00BFFF
RGB 0, 191, 255

Denim
HEX #6F8FAF
RGB 111, 143, 175

Duck
HEX #007791
RGB 0, 119, 145

Egyptian blue
HEX #1434A4
RGB 20, 52, 164

Electric blue
HEX #7DF9FF
RGB 125, 249, 255

Fluorescent
HEX #15F4EE
RGB 21, 244, 238

Glaucous
HEX #6082B6
RGB 96, 130, 182

Ice
HEX #99FFFF
RGB 153, 255, 255

Imperial
HEX #005A92
RGB 0, 90, 146

Independence
HEX #005A92
RGB 0, 90, 146

Indigo dye
HEX #00416A
RGB 0, 65, 106

Lapis Lazuli
HEX #26619C
RGB 38, 97, 156

Light blue
HEX #ADD8E6
RGB 173, 216, 230

Light sky
HEX #87CEFA
RGB 135, 206, 250

Magic blue
HEX #0077C0
RGB 0, 119, 192

Marian blue
HEX #E1EBEE
RGB 225, 235, 238

Midnight blue
HEX #191970
RGB 25, 25, 112

Millennium
HEX #002244
RGB 0, 34, 68

Morning blue
HEX #8DA399
RGB 141, 163, 153

Munsell blue
HEX #0093AF
RGB 0, 147, 175

Navy
HEX #000080
RGB 0, 0, 128

Neon
HEX #4D4DFF
RGB 77, 77, 255

Non-Photo blue
HEX #A4DDED
RGB 164, 221, 237

Ocean
HEX #009DC4
RGB 0, 157, 196

Olympic
HEX #008ECC
RGB 0, 142, 204

Pacific
HEX #1CA9C9
RGB 28, 169, 201

Pastel blue
HEX #A7C7E7
RGB 167, 199, 231

Peacock
HEX #005F69
RGB 0, 95, 105

Periwinkle
HEX #CCCCFF
RGB 204, 204, 255

Phthalo
HEX #000F89
RGB 0, 15, 137

Polynesian blue
HEX #224C98
RGB 34, 76, 152

Powder blue
HEX #B6D0E2
RGB 182, 208, 226

Prussian blue
HEX #003153
RGB 0, 49, 83

Queen blue
HEX #436B95
RGB 67, 107, 149

Resolution blue
HEX #002387
RGB 0, 35, 135

Robin egg
HEX #96DED1
RGB 150, 222, 209

Royal blue
HEX #41690
RGB 65, 105, 225

Sapphire
HEX #0F52BA
RGB 15, 82, 186

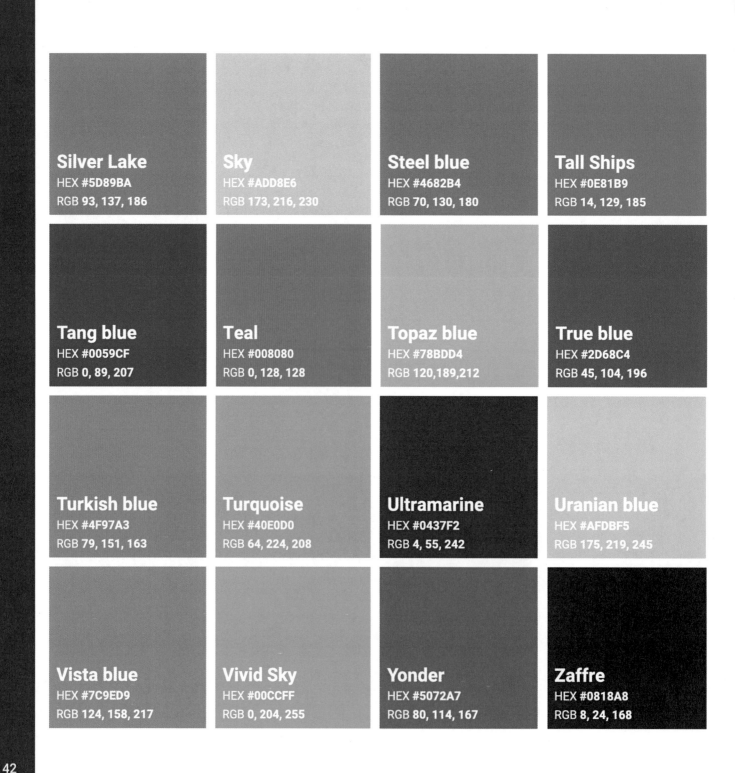

Silver Lake
HEX #5D89BA
RGB 93, 137, 186

Sky
HEX #ADD8E6
RGB 173, 216, 230

Steel blue
HEX #4682B4
RGB 70, 130, 180

Tall Ships
HEX #0E81B9
RGB 14, 129, 185

Tang blue
HEX #0059CF
RGB 0, 89, 207

Teal
HEX #008080
RGB 0, 128, 128

Topaz blue
HEX #78BDD4
RGB 120,189,212

True blue
HEX #2D68C4
RGB 45, 104, 196

Turkish blue
HEX #4F97A3
RGB 79, 151, 163

Turquoise
HEX #40E0D0
RGB 64, 224, 208

Ultramarine
HEX #0437F2
RGB 4, 55, 242

Uranian blue
HEX #AFDBF5
RGB 175, 219, 245

Vista blue
HEX #7C9ED9
RGB 124, 158, 217

Vivid Sky
HEX #00CCFF
RGB 0, 204, 255

Yonder
HEX #5072A7
RGB 80, 114, 167

Zaffre
HEX #0818A8
RGB 8, 24, 168

GREEN

NATURE

HEALING

FRESHNESS

QUALITY

WEALTH

HARMONY

POSSESSIVE

HOPE

FERTILITY

GROWTH

REJUVINATING

India green
HEX #138808
RGB 19, 136, 8

Android
HEX #3DDC84
RGB 61, 220, 132

Apple green
HEX #8AB800
RGB 138, 184, 0

Army green
HEX #454B1B
RGB 69, 75, 27

Artichoke
HEX #8F9779
RGB 143, 151, 121

Asparagus
HEX #87A96B
RGB 135,169,107

Avocado
HEX #568203
RGB 86, 130, 3

Bitter lime
HEX #BFFF00
RGB 191, 255, 0

Bottle
HEX #006A4E
RGB 0, 106, 78

Bright green
HEX #AAFF00
RGB 170, 255, 0

Cadmium
HEX #006B3C
RGB 0, 107, 60

Camouflage
HEX #78866B
RGB 120, 134, 107

Caribbean green
HEX #00CC99
RGB 0, 204, 153

Celadon
HEX #AFE1AF
RGB 175, 225, 175

Chartreuse
HEX #7FFF00
RGB 127, 255, 0

Chetwode
HEX #F0FFF0
RGB 240, 255, 240

Christmas green
HEX #00873E
RGB 0, 135, 62

Corn green
HEX #71A92C
RGB 113, 169, 44

Dark green
HEX #023020
RGB 2, 48, 32

Dark spring
HEX #177245
RGB 23, 114, 69

Deep jungle
HEX #004B49
RGB 0, 75, 73

Dollar bill
HEX #85BB65
RGB 133, 187, 101

Emerald
HEX #50C878
RGB 80, 200, 120

Erin
HEX #00FF40
RGB 0, 255, 64

Eucalyptus
HEX #5F8575
RGB 95, 133, 117

Fern green
HEX #4F7942
RGB 79, 121, 66

Forest
HEX #228B22
RGB 34, 139, 34

Fun
HEX #007848
RGB 0, 120, 72

Gin
HEX #D8E4BC
RGB 216, 228, 188

GO green
HEX #00AB66
RGB 0, 171, 102

Green lizard
HEX #A7F432
RGB 167, 244, 50

Harlequin
HEX #3FFF00
RGB 63, 255, 0

Hooker's green
HEX #49796B
RGB 73, 121, 107

Hunter green
HEX #355E3B
RGB 53, 94, 59

Iguana
HEX #71BC78
RGB 113, 188, 120

Inchworm
HEX #B2EC5D
RGB 178, 236, 93

India green
HEX #138808
RGB 19, 136, 8

Jade green
HEX #00A36C
RGB 0, 163, 108

Jungle green
HEX #2AAA8A
RGB 42, 170, 138

Kelly green
HEX #4CBB17
RGB 76, 187, 23

Laurel
HEX #A9BA9D
RGB 169, 186, 157

Light green
HEX #90EE90
RGB 144, 238, 144

Lime
HEX #C0FF00
RGB 192, 255, 0

Lime green
HEX #32CD32
RGB 50, 205, 50

Limerick
HEX #9DC209
RGB 157, 194, 9

Malachite
HEX #0BDA51
RGB 11, 218, 81

Mantis
HEX #74C365
RGB 116, 195, 101

Maximum green
HEX #4C9A2A
RGB 76, 154, 42

Midnight green
HEX #004953
RGB 0, 73, 83

Mint green
HEX #3EB489
RGB 62, 180, 137

Moss green
HEX #8A9A5B
RGB 138, 154, 91

Myrtle
HEX #21421E
RGB 33, 66, 30

Napier
HEX #2A8000
RGB 42, 128, 0

Neon green
HEX #0FFF50
RGB 15, 255, 80

Olive
HEX #708238
RGB 112, 130, 56

Olivine
HEX #9AB973
RGB 154, 185, 115

Paris green
HEX #00A693
RGB 0, 166, 147

Pastel green
HEX #C1E1C1
RGB 193, 225, 193

Peridot
HEX #B4C424
RGB 180, 196, 36

Persian green
HEX #00A693
RGB 0, 166, 147

Pine
HEX #01796F
RGB 1, 121, 111

Pine needle
HEX #454D32
RGB 69, 77, 50

Pistachio
HEX #93C572
RGB 147, 197, 114

Reseda green
HEX #6C7C59
RGB 108, 124, 89

Sage green
HEX #8A9A5B
RGB 138, 154, 91

Screamin' green
HEX #76FF7A
RGB 118, 255, 122

Sea green
HEX #2E8B57
RGB 46, 139, 87

Seafoam green
HEX #9FE2BF
RGB 159, 226, 191

Shamrock
HEX #009E60
RGB 0, 158, 96

Slimy
HEX #299617
RGB 41, 150, 23

Spring bud
HEX #A7FC00
RGB 167, 252, 0

Spring green
HEX #00FF7F
RGB 0, 255, 127

Swamp
HEX #A8C090
RGB 168, 192, 144

Tea green
HEX #D0F0C0
RGB 208, 240, 192

Thyme
HEX #5EDC1F
RGB 94, 220, 31

Tropical rainforest
HEX #00755E
RGB 0, 117, 94

Turquoise green
HEX #A0D6B4
RGB 160, 214, 180

Verdigris
HEX #40B5AD
RGB 64, 181, 173

Viridian
HEX #40826D
RGB 64, 130, 109

Volt
HEX #CEFF00
RGB 206, 255, 0

Xanadu
HEX #738678
RGB 115, 134, 120

BROWN

STRENGTH

RUGGED

TRUSTWORTHY

SIMPLE

COZY

STABLE

COMFORTABLE

BITTER

RUSTIC

ORDINARY

WARN

Camel
HEX **#C19A6B**
RGB **193, 154, 107**

Almond
HEX #EADDCA
RGB 234, 221, 202

Antique brass
HEX #CD9575
RGB 205, 149, 117

Auburn
HEX #A52A2A
RGB 165, 42, 42

Baked bread
HEX #DACBA9
RGB 218, 203, 169

Bamboo
HEX #E3DEC6
RGB 227, 222, 198

Beaver
HEX #9F8170
RGB 159, 129, 112

Bisque
HEX #FFE4C4
RGB 255, 228, 196

Bistre
HEX #3D2B1F
RGB 61, 43, 31

Bole
HEX #79443B
RGB 121, 68, 59

Bone
HEX #E3DAC9
RGB 227, 218, 201

Bronze
HEX #CD7F32
RGB 205, 127, 50

Brown sugar
HEX #AF6E4D
RGB 175, 110, 77

Buff
HEX #DAA06D
RGB 218, 160, 109

Burlywood
HEX #DEB887
RGB 222, 184, 135

Burnt sienna
HEX #AF6E4D
RGB 175, 110, 77

Burnt Umber
HEX #6E260E
RGB 110, 38, 14

Cafe au lait
HEX #A67B5B
RGB 166, 123, 91

Cafe noir
HEX #4B3621
RGB 75, 54, 33

Camel
HEX #C19A6B
RGB 193, 154, 107

Caramel
HEX #C68E17
RGB 198, 142, 23

Chai
HEX #B1832F
RGB 177, 131, 47

Chamoisee
HEX #A0785A
RGB 160, 120, 90

Chicory
HEX #A78658
RGB 167, 134, 88

Chocolate
HEX #7B3F00
RGB 123, 63, 0

Cinnamon
HEX #D27D2D
RGB 210, 125, 45

Coconut
HEX #965A3E
RGB 150, 90, 62

Coffee
HEX #6F4E37
RGB 111, 78, 55

Cognac
HEX #834333
RGB 131, 67, 51

Copper
HEX #B87333
RGB 184, 115, 51

Cotton
HEX #FAF4D4
RGB 250, 244, 212

Coyote brown
HEX #81613C
RGB 129, 97, 60

Croissant
HEX #C4AB86
RGB 196, 171, 134

Dark brown
HEX #5C4033
RGB 92, 64, 51

Dark tan
HEX #988558
RGB 152, 133, 88

Deer
HEX #BA8759
RGB 186, 135, 89

Desert Sand
HEX #EDC9AF
RGB 237, 201, 175

Dirt
HEX #9B7653
RGB 155, 118, 83

Earth yellow
HEX #E1A95F
RGB 225, 169, 95

Fallow
HEX #C19A6B
RGB 193, 154, 107

Fawn
HEX #E5AA70
RGB 229, 170, 112

Field drab
HEX #6C541E
RGB 108, 84, 30

Fortune cookie
HEX #E0C5A1
RGB 224, 197, 161

Fulvous
HEX #E48400
RGB 228, 132, 0

Ginger
HEX #B06500
RGB 176, 101, 0

Golden brown
HEX #966919
RGB 150, 105, 25

Honey brown
HEX #BA9238
RGB 186, 146, 56

Kobicha
HEX #6B4423
RGB 107, 68, 35

Lace
HEX #EAE3D2
RGB 234, 227, 210

Light brown
HEX #C4A484
RGB 196, 164, 132

Liver
HEX #674C47
RGB 103, 76, 71

Maple syrup
HEX #BB9351
RGB 187, 147, 81

Mars
HEX #AD6242
RGB 173, 98, 66

Medium brown
HEX #7F5112
RGB 127, 81, 18

Mocha
HEX #967969
RGB 150, 121, 105

Nude
HEX #F2D2BD
RGB 242, 210, 189

Ochre
HEX #CC7722
RGB 204, 119, 34

Olive green
HEX #808000
RGB 128, 128, 0

Oxblood
HEX #4A0404
RGB 74, 4, 4

Raw umber
HEX #826644
RGB 130, 102, 68

Rosy brown
HEX #BC8F8F
RGB 188, 143, 143

Rufous
HEX #A81C07
RGB 168, 28, 7

Russet
HEX #80461B
RGB 128, 70, 27

Rust
HEX #B7410E
RGB 183, 65, 14

Saddle brown
HEX #8B4513
RGB 139, 69, 19

Sand
HEX #F6D7B0
RGB 246, 215, 176

Sandy brown
HEX #F4A460
RGB 244, 164, 96

Seal brown
HEX #59260B
RGB 89, 38, 11

Sepia
HEX #704214
RGB 112, 66, 20

Sienna
HEX #A0522D
RGB 160, 82, 45

Sinopia
HEX #CB410B
RGB 203, 65, 11

Tan
HEX #D2B48C
RGB 210, 180, 140

Taupe
HEX #483C32
RGB 72, 60, 50

Tawny
HEX #CD5700
RGB 205, 87, 0

Tumbleweed
HEX #DEAA88
RGB 222, 170, 136

Tuscan brown
HEX #6F4E37
RGB 111, 78, 55

Umber
HEX #635147
RGB 99, 81, 71

Walnut brown
HEX #5C5248
RGB 92, 82, 72

Wenge
HEX #645452
RGB 100, 84, 82

Wheat
HEX #F5DEB3
RGB 245, 222, 179

Wood
HEX #C19A6B
RGB 193, 154, 107

BLACK

FORMALITY

DRAMATIC

ELEGANCE

AUTHORITY

SOBRIETY

RESPECT

SERIOUSNESS

POWER

MYSTERY

COLDNESS

SOPHISTICATION

Abbey
HEX #494F55
RGB 73, 79, 85

Aesthetic black
HEX #1C1C1E
RGB 28, 28, 30

Alien black
HEX #1A2228
RGB 26, 34, 40

Arsenic
HEX #3B444B
RGB 59, 68, 75

Ash gray
HEX #666362
RGB 102, 99, 98

Basalt black
HEX #4D423E
RGB 77, 66, 62

Black Bean
HEX #3D0C02
RGB 61, 12, 2

Black cat
HEX #413839
RGB 65, 56, 57

Black chocolate
HEX #1B1811
RGB 27, 24, 17

Black coral
HEX #54626F
RGB 84, 98, 111

Black cow
HEX #4C4646
RGB 76, 70, 70

Black denim
HEX #191C27
RGB 25, 28, 39

Black eel
HEX #463E3F
RGB 70, 62, 63

Black grain
HEX #2C2C2A
RGB 44, 44, 42

Black hole
HEX #060605
RGB 6, 6, 5

Black leather
HEX #253529
RGB 37, 53, 41

Black olive
HEX #3B3C36
RGB 59, 60, 54

Black pearl
HEX #0E161A
RGB 14, 22, 26

Black rock
HEX #010127
RGB 1, 1, 39

Black Truffle
HEX #463D3E
RGB 70, 61, 62

Blackberry
HEX #3A3A38
RGB 58, 58, 56

Cafe americano
HEX #362819
RGB 54, 40, 25

Carbon
HEX #333333
RGB 51, 51, 51

Charcoal
HEX #36454F
RGB 54, 69, 79

Cool black
HEX #151922
RGB 21, 25, 34

Cynical black
HEX #171717
RGB 23, 23, 23

Dark jungle
HEX #1A2421
RGB 26, 36, 33

Dark raisin
HEX #1A0F0F
RGB 26, 15, 15

Dim gray
HEX #696969
RGB 105, 105, 105

Dull black
HEX #161616
RGB 22, 22, 22

Ebony
HEX #555D50
RGB 85, 93, 80

Eerie black
HEX #1B1B1B
RGB 27, 27, 27

Electric black
HEX #292929
RGB 41, 41, 41

Gothic grape
HEX #120321
RGB 18, 3, 33

Granite
HEX #676767
RGB 103, 103, 103

Gray cloud
HEX #B6B6B4
RGB 182, 182, 180

Grease
HEX #1A1F21
RGB 26, 31, 33

Gray wolf
HEX #504A4B
RGB 80, 74, 75

Gunmetal
HEX #2C3539
RGB 44, 53, 57

Iridium
HEX #3D3C3A
RGB 61, 60, 58

Iron black
HEX #343432
RGB 52, 52, 50

Ivory black
HEX #231F20
RGB 35, 31, 32

Jade
HEX #000302
RGB 0, 3, 2

Jet black
HEX #343434
RGB 52, 52, 52

Kombu green
HEX #354230
RGB 53, 66, 48

Lamp black
HEX #2E473B
RGB 46, 71, 59

Leather
HEX #282829
RGB 40, 40, 41

Licorice
HEX #1B1212
RGB 27, 18, 18

Marengo
HEX #4C5866
RGB 76, 88, 102

Matte black
HEX #28282B
RGB 40, 40, 43

Metropolis
HEX #1A1A1A
RGB 26, 26, 26

Midnight
HEX #2B1B17
RGB 43, 27, 23

Nickel
HEX #727472
RGB 114, 116, 114

Night sky
HEX #0C1445
RGB 12, 20, 69

Night shadow
HEX #1C1C1C
RGB 28, 28, 28

Obsidian
HEX #020403
RGB 2, 4, 3

Off black
HEX #595652
RGB 89, 86, 82

Oil
HEX #3B3131
RGB 59, 49, 49

Onyx
HEX #353935
RGB 53, 57, 53

Outer space
HEX #414A4C
RGB 65, 74, 76

Panda black
HEX #3C4748
RGB 60, 71, 72

Peacoat
HEX #2B2E43
RGB 43, 46, 67

Pig iron
HEX #484848
RGB 72, 72, 72

Raisin black
HEX #242124
RGB 36, 33, 36

Raisin
HEX #524144
RGB 82, 65, 68

Reflecting pond
HEX #203E4A
RGB 32, 62, 64

Retro black
HEX #1F201F
RGB 31, 32, 31

Scorpion
HEX #5E5E5E
RGB 94, 94, 94

Sepia black
HEX #2B0202
RGB 43, 2, 2

Shadows
HEX #7B7A72
RGB 123, 122, 114

Slate
HEX #26282A
RGB 38, 40, 42

Soot
HEX #160D08
RGB 22, 13, 8

Stellar
HEX #23323F
RGB 35, 50, 63

Stormcloud
HEX #4F666A
RGB 79, 102, 106

Tap shoe
HEX #2A2B2D
RGB 42, 43, 45

Turbulent sea
HEX #212A30
RGB 33, 42, 48

Vampire
HEX #565051
RGB 86, 80, 81

Void
HEX #010207
RGB 1, 2, 7

Winter waves
HEX #102126
RGB 16, 33, 38

Zinnwaldite brown
HEX #2C1608
RGB 44, 22, 8

Made in the USA
Las Vegas, NV
03 May 2024

89467774R10040